Man, Woman and Child

Dr. Delbert Blair

Inner Alchemy's Publishing
Chicago, IL

Copyright © 2015 Dr. Delbert Blair. All rights reserved. No portion of this publication may be copied, reproduced, stored in a retrieval system, reposted, duplicated, or transmitted, in any means, electronic, mechanical, photocopying, recording, or otherwise not known or hereafter to become known without the express written permission of InnerAlchemys.com, Inner Alchemy's, Inner Alchemy's Publishing.

First Edition

ISBN 978-0-9961266-0-1

Any trade names, trademarks, service marks, etc. mentioned in this publication are for identification only. Therefore, any specific company or product mentioned is owned by their respective owner and not by Inner Alchemy's Publishing. Further, the company or product mentioned neither owns, endorses, nor has heard of Inner Alchemy's Publishing. By stating this, we can avoid printing the ®, ™, ©, etc. marks that we might otherwise have to place throughout the text.

The publisher does not participate in, endorse, or have any authority or responsibility concerning private business transactions between our authors and the public.

Published by
    Inner Alchemy's Publishing (Inner Alchemy's)
    332 S. Michigan Ave.
    Ste 1032-C141
    Chicago, IL 60604 4434

    info@inneralchemys.com
    www.inneralchemys.com

Printed in the United States of America

Dedication

All Re-Incarnates to planet Terrestris! Inner, on, or extra-terrestrials, special advanced elder souls, walk in's, crystals, star seeds, guides, angel's etc.

May the knowledge gained in this present-now, give you the wisdom to free your soul for the future-then! As you seek higher vibratory dimensions and become the gods you want to be.

From the lessons you've learned from trial and error, success and failure, prayer and meditation. It is no accident that you are living on this planetary classroom as she is receiving a double promotion from third dimension (kindergarten) to 5th dimension (graduate school).

Congratulations! You're earning it, may the creator continue to bless you!

CONTENTS

The Real Man, Woman, and Child Lecture Part 1 1

The Real Man, Woman, and Child Lecture Part 2 13

The Real Man, Woman, and Child Lecture Part 3 18

The Real Man, Woman, and Child Lecture Part 4 26

Universal Creator's Prayer 32

The Real Man, Woman, and Child Lecture

Part 1

We are going to get very deep tonight! We are going to get into a subject matter that may be somewhat troublest to some, and you are going to hear a few comments that are going to be way out. You're going to hear some suggestions that may be way out. Having talked with some of you individually, what I used to consider way out is now commonplace, because many of you are dealing with the thoughts of aliens and interfacings here, and al kinds of genetic splicing.

So, although at one time, the lecture was phenomenal, now it's just run-of-the-mill: it's just something else that would be good to have in your arsenal, to oppose or to understand what either threatens you or tends to work with you.

I make no bones about the contents. I simply research and I present it to you the same way. We're going to start off with the woman lecture and that's because women run everything anyway, right? How many of you say women run everything? Don't you even do it! I don't even want to see these hands. They are starting to raise theirs up too. I saw you. Let's just say that probably some of the most interesting products and subjects on this planet are women. Isn't that a terrible way to address the female gender? But you are if you are a female. Simply because females, I think, are the worst critics of other females on Earth. They will tear a man apart but then they will give some reason why: a woman made him like that or a lack of a woman made him like that. But when it comes to interaction with each other, they can become terrible. Hopefully some of that is changing, but as you will see tonight, there are times in which females do ally with each other. You do come together as one in the face of some things men might say or do. OJ Simpson excluded.

What I am going to say is simply this: the time we are living in is a time when knowledge and wisdom will be manifest. Without true understanding it is impossible to manifest complete wisdom, because there's lack of knowledge. I let the chips fall where they may.

I did some research and it stated that "woman" was an adult female human being. I don't think we have got a problem with that at all. Is there anyone who has a problem with that definition? Alright, we are together, at least at the start. It says that "womanhood" was a time or condition of being a woman. It makes sense to me and I don't think there is a big deal there either. We may have an interesting interface with the following one, because it says that "girl" is a female child or young unmarried woman, or, at one time, the word "girl" meant young boy. That one kind of grabbed me, I had to look for some other references. You know, when you get to your third different definition, for whatever the original was... I said it was interesting. It is going to become more interesting as we move on.

I looked biblically because many people feel that they understand the Bible, and feel that whatever is in the Bible is adequate and true. Thus, consequently it stated that the rib from Adam was created, to give man a helpmate, which referred to as a woman. Created from Adam's rib to be a helpmate to man. I didn't know if it meant "help meet the bills" or "help meet somebody at the train station" or what, but it did say "helpmate". I'm sure you have a better interpretation of it than I do. In my ignorance, I questioned what that was. With all of that around, I then began to look even deeper into the phenomenal set of cells and set of personalities there are in females and I found something which I know all of you will agree with: that woman is indeed, bless her heart, the weaker sex. That woman is, in general, a prime example of what a womb-man can be, and that, of course, men are obviously much smarter because of the brain structure, and yet we still try to be compatible. Do you have any problems with these last three statements? A lot of problems. Why did I think that some women may have a problem with that? Are there any men with any problems with what I just said? One man. Well, you don't count, you are just one man, with a problem, ok. All the rest of the men did not raise their hands. Alright, he is just saying that because he wants you to buy his tapes. I know what it is. Well, I think I can give you proof, even though I said that may be an exaggeration. But if you can back up an exaggeration, it may become truth. So, let's see if I can back that up. I want you to listen carefully before you pass judgment now, because I'm now going to show you why I said that. I think you may agree with me at the end, or maybe not.

Throughout the world there are more widows, than widowers. There are more women 100 and over than there are men 100 and over. The female body on a worldwide racial consideration retains the characteristics of youth larger than males do. Less, or at least fewer women have hardening of the arteries, most women, again, have a tendency to adjust blood pressure a little bit quicker and faster than men, if you will. And the incidence of ulcers is much lighter in women than in men. Let me say, however, that's changing as women are beginning to develop ulcers, and I can't understand why on a per capita racial by states in the United States, up to 60% as fast as men. There is more heart failure and epilepsy in men than in women, and when it comes to retaining breath in using oxygen, women are much less easier to suffocate and are able to retain their ability for longer than men. Women can endure cold weather on a general basis better than men, and at higher altitudes, where there is 18% less oxygen and, of course, they don't know without oxygen products women survive much better. Women who live on the Andes Mountains and, of course, all women must live in the Andes Mountains, can carry heavier loads than men, because oxidation capacity being stronger, the muscle texture and tenure is stronger.

Just because I'm going about half way through this, I guess you can see how I am supportive of my original premise and statement. You do see how I am backing this up, right? How many of you agree that I'm backing it up? None? Well, I think I'm doing a good job at backing it up. Let me go on, maybe I haven't said enough, let me go on with this a bit.

The female brain not only has a finer texture and has a more complex organization than that of the man, but relative to the overall bodyweight it is one – quarter heavier. There are fewer females, well that's not true, baby miscarriages, than there are boy or male baby miscarriages. They carry more girls than boys to term successfully. During childhood, the female is mentally superior to males, the female also has a larger thyroid gland, which has three lobes to the male's two-globe-gland. You must remember that because it is going to have an important bearing when we really get heavy here.

Now, the three secret glands of females are the one that has been misquoted or not properly given its place, the three lobed thyroid gland. The two lobed thyroid male glands. A girl of 7, because of the high concentration of the thyroid hormone thyroxin, has a brain capacity that a boy doesn't get until he is 14. Strong mental and physical women conceive girl babies almost all the time. In fact, 99% of zygotes are females when formed. With all that, I have proven without a shadow of a doubt, all of the things that I stated and stressed at the beginning. Right....right.

As a man it makes me feel much better to say that I backed up, even If I haven't. The whole point is that the ladies seem to have a lot on the male body, the male brain up until a certain thing begins to happen. Then most of the things I began to talk about reversed.

The problems start with the word "men". Menstruation or the menses. I will refer to it as the menses. Menstruating women loose calcium, thyroxin, iodine, phosphorus, lethicin, vitamin E, B1, B6, B12, B15, magnesium, iron, copper, zinc. And some of the loss occurs two weeks before the menses start, in what is called "locaria". Now, just to say, that may not make an impact. It should. Just in case, let me explain a couple of things that I mentioned. Calcium, for instance, not only in teeth and so stabilizes the nervous system. Without Calcium, the nervous system can't function correctly. Phosphorus is found in all healthy normal cells. Iodine, the lack of which or overabundance of which leads to what we call hyperthyroidism. Even though it is not the master gland, it affects everything from the throat down and a few from the throat up again. The growth and maintenance of the body, through the growth and maintenance of the thyroid gland is a must, and interesting enough, the thyroid gland tends to swell during menstruation. There's a reason Science has gone so far to prove that the birth of congenital idiots increases as the iodine supply decreases. A type of sea iodine found in algae and lichen family is decreasing. In this case, we have all been blessed, because when it rains it pours. We can all go out and buy iodine salt. But understand, in many cases iodine is from a land base consumption, and land plants are not as rich in chlorophyll, and therefore their mineral value does not have as much energy in them as a seed vegetative.

Now, we accept this concept of menstruation as something that is done for the woman as decreed by nature, when one is born female, and that is all there has to do with it. Let me state that this is not exactly the case. There are women throughout the world and even now who do not menstruate or never did menstruate, and in the sense of a tribe or nation, has profundity or the propensity to generally not menstruate. Most Hindu women do not menstruate. One of the last ones, that was very much proclaimed for her no need for such, was Handor Ghandi. Most ancient African woman did not menstruate. Belcus, of ancient Greek, and Salfow, of the ancient Greek, and oracles of the Delphi, who were all Grecian women that were replaced in half by men, prophets if you would, people who could look into the future and guide Grecian society, did not menstruate, Hapatia being one of them, Korena being another, the Amazon women, the tutonic women, the female Gaulic women, the West African Wautichitas, the West African Bosemans, and the Adambes of the Congo. None of these women believed in menstruation nor did their bodies mense or go through a mense. Why is it that they become the exception? They also grow stronger, taller, have more psychic skills, and a higher ability to bring in new births without a lot of drugs. They are stronger and they do not menstruate. Obviously again, if they brought in births, how is that possible when they did not undergo menstruation?

We found that there has been a lot of misinterpretation from some so called Holy books, holy sacred books, and a lot of purposeful - well, how can I put it, changings of what was taught at one time, by the final agenda called "men heading up organizations" like churches and medical societies for certain purposes. Maybe that's a challenge that you won't accept, but let us look into this whole idea again. Women have been told and they have traced it back to biblical interpretation by many prophets, priests, ministers, and reverends that menses are an unclean issue that was necessary and that women should be ostracized from society or tribe and that it was a sign of her uncleanliness.

We have also been told that it is the breakdown of the uterine walls, endometriosis being when the uterine walls is very effected, breaking down of the egg before it is fertilized. Consequently, this is why the issue is necessary. I state that none of these things may be true. But I can state anything: it is not enough that I state it. It's for the best we begin to look more and more into this whole subject matter, if you would.

With the advent of monogamy, and in many cases the ancients were a system of growth, the church needed people to hold onto, it wanted a whole family because not only then does the church become stronger in number, but also the tiding and support was probably more ingrained. They also proffered this idea that the woman should be separated from the tribe during this time, and this was something that was to be frowned upon and was something that therefore showed that a woman is less than a man. I state that it is not a cleansing of the process at all, being just the partial deterioration of the female unfertilized egg. Not only do women undergo the menses, but that's our subject - and I hope again that you are adult enough to deal with this tonight. We're going to have a lot of fun tonight. You will be able to discuss with me later on all that you would like.

There is something called on the streets – again, scientifically called locaria, or the whites: a kataro condition of the womb and an inflammation of the uterine lining, much as endometriosis, that starts there too and, I state, is one of the reasons that causes menstruation. During this phase, locaria, not menstruating women, suffer 2- 3 weeks prior to the start of the menses, which will continue for 2 weeks and usually at least three days. This means that the female is subject to a constant loss of very interesting blood plasma and fluids. Let me explain to some of you, who think that it is smart to laugh at locaria and feel that it something that is not detrimental. Let me tell you what's inside of the locuric fluid. Prior to the menses or after the menses, the fluids lost in locaria are composed of important vital substances such as lipoids, alkali lactates, and natural sodium, potassium, sodium carbonate, calcium, and brain and nerve foods, highly rich in lethicin and phosphotal kolin. The mucous corpuscles present in locaria in reality are not mucous corpuscles at all, they are what we call "hemoglobin capable", simply meaning that they are on their way to becoming red blood corpuscles capable of carrying oxygen. Oxygen, which, if you have been to any of these two lectures at all, I'd tell you don't get enough of it ever: it is almost impossible to get enough oxygen on this planet, faced with the stress and hydrocarbons and the radiation that we are. So, all of these are potentially human blood cells, red hemoglobin capable of oxygenating the body, which are being lost before they can even be formed, and then comes the menses themselves. Any wonder that anyone, such as the females, wouldn't be irritable, in fact dizzy, possibly anemic, and grow old and show the signs of aging with gray hairs and wrinkled skin even faster if they were to be losing all that 4 to 5 weeks out of a 30 to 31 day period. And some women honestly go through that: I hope you don't know any of them and I hope you are not one of them, because they are heck to be around, if that's the case. And what can you expect, if a person is actually losing hemoglobin on a regular basis? I state this is not a natural condition and it is not my big ego that says this. I have done research on those who have done the research and in the little bit of research that I have done, I have to agree with what these aghost doctors and medicine people have reached a term to understand. In addition, it is proposed that if a female could stop these things, both locaria and the menses for no more than 24 hours, then a female could have a capability of producing and bearing a child through term without a male being around.

There is in history, if you do the research again, a theory called the ovist theory. It is spelled o-v-i-s-t and pronounced ah-vist. The ovist theory was proven by a professor, Jock Loeweb, of Stanford University back in the 50s. The ovist theory states that the embryo develops from the egg alone and does not require spermatozoa to begin promulgation of mitosis. In other words, a woman can impregnate herself and bring forth to term, without a male being around producing the male spermatozoa. The prevailing medical theory now is called epigenisis and, I state through these other researchers that epigenesis is not proven necessary, and is yet what everybody now in the heterogeneous makeup in the United States pretty much believes in.

Also, however, this also brings out some other theories. You might accept some of those, and yet might not accept the latter one, which states that you cannot get a man from a man, you cannot get a woman from a man, but you can get a man from a woman, and you can get a woman from a woman. This is what I propose the old church heads have to change, having to read from the books that talk about it and having to read the book you refer to as the bible. Well, you see, males cannot reproduce themselves and without females, the species phylum of man as we understand him wouldn't be in existence.

And there was a time when that species was threatened. Ok. Now we get to the light stuff or, should I say, the heavier contention. DR. Edward Bhishof, an M.D., stated what is called "the modern acceptance of the theory of apenasis", that started in 1864, for those of you who are taking notes, 1854. That means that the zygote and uterine development by the union of sperm and egg is what Bhishof's theory was about. His theory has been accepted. It is only a theory.

For centuries, people have believed in and some people still believe in parthenogenesis. Parthenogenesis. In the ancient Parthenon in Greece, there was a product of a culture that believed in parthenogenesis, having been given to them by some ancients called Akadians and Atuvains, who believed in the parthenogenic receptor of the human egg. The female was only one of the regenerators of that and when that theory failed to captivate the masses, then the thought of epigenesis occurred.

But before that time, it was understood that the complete cyclic birth for a God man had to be parthenogenic. That was their belief. In the year of 1955, four very prominent British doctors of medicine, Dr. Stanley Bell Fourlyn, Dr. Bernard Camber, Dr. David Wine Williams, and Dr. A. E Muwau, all studied 10 cases of virgin births and agreed that in some strange way, indeed, parthenogenesis had to have happened. The most famous case study was that of Emma Marie Jones. She was a German woman who became impregnated during the Blitzkrieg time in 1944 at Hitler's Germany. This happened at the height of the war and this woman was encased, entombed, if you would, in a castle. Fortunately, there was a stream underground and there were lots of canned provisions for over 15 months. She was found to have been in her seventh month of pregnancy when rescued. That has never been explained by the so-called medical sciences of this day, but was a common occurrence, especially under the stress of entombment, in the ancient times. But we will look into that later.

If the ovist theory is to be even profligated and definitely accepted, then we must begin to see what kind of conceptuality brought this into being, how we can begin to say that this may have to be the way and the meaning of the human species on Earth. We see, in studying classical history and looking into what the ancients have said, that a lot of different practices go on and a lot of different worships are coming about or beginning to be dropped. The question has been - you have heard it proposed before, "which comes first, the chicken or the egg?", and I think that the old axiom was "which came first, the chicken and the egg, or the egg on the chick, or chicken on the egg?"... I ask you for a vote. I want you to raise your hand, if you believe, when I ask it, that the chicken came first, and then I want you to raise your hand if you believe that the egg came first. But I don't want you to raise both hands, nor do I want you to vote twice. K. If you believe that the first creature was the chicken and not the eggs, raise your hand. Ok, roughly around twenty people. Ok, please lower your hands. If you believe it was the egg, please raise your hand. About 31 people. How many did not vote, to be made a fool of, so you're just not going to commit. There you go, you're a trip. Alright, that figures. Alright. Playcators, politicians. Alright. Well, it obviously has to be the chicken. I mean, does it? You know what kind of doubt it could be that it's not the chicken.

Especially, since in 1975, at Stanford University, they connected a vibrational detection censor to an unfertilized egg and got a rhythmic pulsating beat just like that of a human heart. That experiment has been repeated knowingly 230 times with the same results on an unfertilized egg. What is an unfertilized egg? Anyone really intelligent here, really quick? Yes. No rooster around, there was no rooster there. Well what does that do to the chicken and an egg, huh? Not a hen and egg, not a rooster and an egg, but a chicken and an egg. This would possibly mean that there was some kind of life-force in an egg, generated by the female that did not receive the fertilization. A life pulse, huh? Obviously, the thing would be, are there any other species in nature, plant, animal or otherwise that can begin to substantiate that or show the same kind of proclivity? How many of you have ever seen an acorn or cut an acorn in half? Raise your hands. Interesting enough, if you look at that acorn, there is an imprint right there where the seed should be and, in many cases, it looks like a full grown oak tree, there is information before they began to genetically mutate some of your acorns. But they grew naturally to what looks like a big oak tree, which shows where that little seed might grow and what that it might grow into.

Also, the silk moth reproduces itself without mating. In fact, if it mates, it cannot reproduce silk and soon after mating it dies. A lonely aphid, some call it an aphid, I call it an aphid, a little old lonely bug, if you would, reproducing without a mate. And yet the phylum of man can subjugate and conjugate with anything on Earth. The Egyptians, of course a very non – essential, backward, non – pyramid building society, had a very interesting thing: they worshipped almost what is behind me on the wall, the scarab. Most people refer to it as the scarab beetle. The scarab is a very interesting creature, has a 7 year life cycle, and if it does not mate, it reproduces. If it does not mate, it reproduces. Up until that time, it is capable of casting off its skin, borning itself anew, and if it does not mate there is new reproduction, and the first one dies and the other one carries its seed which has to be fertilized by another beetle. The beetle doesn't need a mate for reproduction. Now, that sacred beetle, the good luck charm or the scarab, obviously may now grow in its meaning as to what they were trying to say to us and why they characterized a little insect as being strong and mighty.

I give you food for thought, if the human species is the highest life form on Earth, then isn't it strange that seeds, moths, aphids can do what human cannot do? If you believe in epigenesis only... I state, since nature always shows by sign and nature has nothing to hide from man, because man to nature is a beetle to a planet, then maybe we should look at what nature has said and is saying. All of that simply leads up to a final idea, or may be a commencement idea of who and what we are as humans. And I state the story that they came out with in various books, under the new age concept that is now beginning to surface in research centers and medical facilities throughout the Earth. They will still not share it with the public nor the laity. It says that this is a very old planet and that when life forms began to resemble, they were hermaphrodites or dual seeded androgynous or androgens having males and females on the same plant stem. And that's an interesting word, as you shall see, and at one time there were even etherens or, in other words, there was no solid human form on Earth, yet there was intelligent life in some form. Here is the way the story goes, and I will move on carefully and slowly. And I will tell you now that in the next ten minutes it's going to get very rough, and if some of you feel you cannot bare this kind of stories, you can go and buy some of the products from the back or the table and close your ears.

But if I just made you very hungry for what may be happening, let me finish before you reach a conclusion, let me speak and I'll try to deal with it as scientifically as possible. It's going to get very interesting.

The woman was the first female sex creation that endured the sensation of the hermaphroditic state: in other words, it was that phylum now called a woman that endured the dual sex seed, having two sexes in one. This original person or this original species of human dwells in the heavens of the Earth, or what is called the "etheric vibrations", the much faster vibrations than the physical ones. As the atoms of the planet condense, so did the atoms of this species condense in the lower heavens of the Earth. This condensation lead to a lower and lower vibrational rate within the atomic structure of both the planet and of this species that lived in the heavenly essence of that planet until both became fairly solid. Then the hermaphroditic tendencies, through what is called a coalescence of the chakra centers, changed to an androgenic conception. It's interesting also that the word "androgynous" means having male and female parts on the same plant cluster, but "androgen" has been named by men as being any substance that induces or strengthens masculine characteristics.

The Real Man, Woman, and Child Lecture

Part 2

Such as a male sex hormone. How far have we come? When advanced species, during ancient times, mated with earthen animals, their court resulted in a new offspring, the animal man. The animal portion of their union followed the animal menses which are governed by the moon, and at that time the Earth took on a moon. They were then called hu- man or animal man, lower vibratory creatures of fallen heavens.

Theory number 3: when this advanced species mated with animals on Earth, the act resulted in another fallen energy unit, even lower than the original humans, who at least needed the moon cycle to propagate.

High alkali diets, enzymes, fresh juices, oxygen, and chlorophyll containing foods along with deep breathing and exercise shortens the menses. Most female athletes, circus performers, long distance runners, tennis players tend to slow their menses to no more than one and half days. Most vegetative animals eating white sugar containing females have their menses extended to a 5 to 7 day cycle. Many normal healthy females don't even start menstruating, not even at 19 or 20 years old, and then it comes to the worried parents, the ignorant doctors or the money – hungry doctors bring their menstrual cycles on with intensive efforts, and I won't be so low as to tell you some of the practices to induce menses, but maybe some of you males or females may have heard of them. They can become extremely violent and volatile.

All original zygotes are females when formed, they later change and as our planet has lowered in its vibration now, that is at least 98% true. After 6 – 8 weeks, the male fetus starts to secrete testosterone, otherwise it would have remained a female. Now, please, we are starting getting rough. Listen attentively and take it accordingly: there is no truth until you decide what the truth is. Sometimes a small quantity of testosterone is secreted, just enough to make testes form on the developing embryo, but not enough to utilize proper brain chemistry and pituitary balance, and indigenous homosexuality can be produced. I don't need to repeat that, because you heard it, didn't you? Want to hear this just one more time? Boy, I'm getting psychic! Sometimes a small quantity of testosterone is secreted, just enough to make testes form on the developing embryo, but not enough to utilize proper brain chemistry and pituitary balance, and indigenous homosexuality can be produced.

Birthmarks are the mental impregnations and decreased ability of women to still mark and control vibratory rates of themselves. Dermoid cysts are the underdeveloped cells, starting the first trimester of fetal development, and microscopic examination will verify this fact. Hair, teeth, and nails are there. In many cases, this budding tendency can manifest itself on each side of the dermoid cyst casing, and even become other types of cysts, especially when improper chemical imbalance is maintained due to drugs.

The word "conception" means to conceive mentally. Man descended from woman and circumcision is the artificial means to finalize this separation. The males testes is a woman's descended ovum, encased within the scrotum. You know what's coming next. The male penis is an elongated clitoris. The female fallopian tube, made by Fallopian in 1523, is a male vas deferens gland or urethra duct, which is really an amalgamation of the fallopian tubes. The male prostrate - and this is one of the reasons prostate trouble is on the increase, is an atrophied womb, and every man has the mammary glands of the female and can produce milk if he is normal. The bulbous urethra glands of the male are the equal of the larger so called vestibular glands of women.

Interesting enough, the female thyroid gland with the three lobes allow iodine storage to keep the bulbous urethra gland functioning when men's begin to dehydrate. What you heard is different. What you heard may already be agreed on by some, heard of by many, and now is being considered by you in the audience. I state this is just the start of what have been the fall of man on Earth and the propagation of a new kind of species. All in all, and since we have a man lecture to follow, and a children's lecture to follow it, I gave you the reasons it is possible to reproduce on Earth without the union of sperm and egg.

Now again, before I crack this portion only, and please don't ask me about man and children, we have a whole two lectures coming up about them, I want to give you some research papers and items for those of you who want to correlate that or do it on your own. One is called Dr. Jeremy Cherfas and Dr. John Gribben. Two books by

Professor Hilton Hotema, one "The Physiological Enigma of Woman", the other "The Great Red Dragon". "The Sky People" by Brinsky Lepor Trench, "The Star People" by Brad and Francis Stiger, and "Man the Unknown" by Alexuis Carol.

Open for statements, questions, comments on women only. What a wonderful subject.

Let me ask this again. If we may, I'd like to prepare to get into my second subject tonight, which has been promised, and I want to try and fulfill, whether you agree with me or not, and that's beautiful. That's the man lecture. At this time, boring, if it wasn't for the women running around on this planet. I think some women might choose to exit, if that was the case. I know a lot of men would. So, I'd like to now get into a little discussion, if we will, about men.

It's interesting, like I said before, when I give the "man lecture" I always expect women, when I give the "woman lecture" sometimes I expect men, but when I give the "man, woman and child lecture", we have a fun interesting time. Say that with some exhilaration and happiness in your voice. Yeah, we're going to have a fun time, right. It's interesting too, that at this time in our race for space, at this time in our 1995 calendar year, we have the OJ Simpson trial dangling like a red dragon and a big sword of Damocles over our heads as we are looking at that, and missing so many other much more important events that are happening in our country at an almost frightening pace. But this is the way we do, first with sex, then with race, then with the whole idea of one sex subjugating another.

There is a day called May Day, celebrated throughout Europe, and celebrated a little bit in the United States. It was canceled in celebration a lot. It was stated that it was practiced by communist nations in the country and the whole idea of May Day become one that was political, rather than its original meaning. Its original meaning was taken from what is called May 1st or happy day, happy May Day sometimes referred to as happy day, happy May Day, the rites of spring, and the fertile season. It was the commensuration of the beginning of summer, the turning of spring, and was celebrated by the good ship, the May Flower, the mayflower that grew the maypole, and the may queen.

I began this talk of man to let you understand that it is an old custom celebrated on every continent of the beginning of man or the sequestering of man by woman. Away from the religious and the puritanical, and even the political thought who views the concept to abuse it. I want to get into what the dictionary says about the phylum species called man. It says that "man" is an adult human being. We're starting off in agreement. Right. Hopefully so. I don't see any hands, so alright. It says that "boy" is a male child, before he becomes a man, and at one time the word "girl" meant "young boy". Now that's just about what we heard about, or what I studied about "girl" and "young".

The Real Man, Woman, and Child Lecture
Part 3

Why has this nomenclature changed? What is it that has made the word "boy" mean "girl" and the word "girl" mean "boy"? Or was it like I alleged at the end of the woman lecture? The word "patriarch" means "a father or head male of a family or tribe", and in the Christian bible, of course, Abraham, Isaac, and Jacob, were examples of patriarchal or patriarcholsy. We presently live and for some time have lived under a patriarchal society, or male ruled society here in the United States, or male ruled Caucasoid dominant. The bible says that Adam was the first man and that the lord God did create him, and that he placed him in a seemingly tropical paradise. Because he might have felt lonely, God made for him other animals and a help mate, which was "womb–man". Because of this emphasis placed on men by the lord–god, religions and nations and political societies have accepted this planet venerated man, and the church says that he is the divine and right for the ruler of all things, and that they were made under him for him to control.

Now some things have happened in our society, which threaten the male. Instead of a "mail man", we now have a "mail person", and I know how you say it but it's spelled m-a-i-l. Well, at one point and time, "mail" really stood for "male", because there were very few letter carriers that were females. That's changed in the last forty years. Instead of "chairman" of the board, there is now a "chairperson". The "congressman" is a "representative", "mankind" is now "human being", and a "police officer" is now an "officer of the law", and you understand all the things that have come into being over the last fifteen years. Believe it or not, this has changed over the last fifteen years. This is not an old subjugated thing.

We were very patriarchal here, not only on Earth, but especially in this country for a long time. We have homosexuality rearing its sexual head, and we now have AIDS threatening homosexuality. We now have all kinds of division of mind concerning who and what is right and what man is, and I say, because of all this, once you begin to question your thought and your concept, you begin to change the presence that is around you. Now, whether it was the chicken and the egg that the thought had to be changed on, and the air and consciousness that we exist in or whether or not as we change, we change the air and consciousness around us, is up to you to choose. But man has begun to change and the word "man" is understood as definitely changing. Everything that I stated in the woman lecture to save some time pretty much holds true in the man lecture, especially as it is associated with women and the women lecture. One thing with the ravages of old age with ulcers, diabetes, and heart attacks and so on and so forth, it is becoming hard for either sex to exist well and man on Earth feels now he is somewhat threatened.

I state, since it was brought out before and I was going to skirt this, but I won't, I'll tell this now, especially since the questions of biblical theology was mentioned, I'll look at this and interpret it another way. Some of you who are Hebrew Israelites already agree with it. Some of you, Islamic, agree to part of this and I'll run through this briefly and then we will see if we need to go over it again. In the first chapter of the Genesis, in the 26th verse, God said "let us make man in our image after our likeness and let them have dominion over etc.", and in Genesis 26th verse it then says "so God created man, and in his own image, in the image of God created male and female". We have here a God creating a male and female at the same time and then calling them mutually "man". Later, a Lord-God and the two terms are used individually, creating another man and calling him Adam. And this is where the trouble really starts with the modern theologists. Preferably, the theologists are calling it "the second creation" or "Adam two" or colloquially "Adam 12's offspring". We have to then look at one basic thing, the Hebrew word for Adam, which means "red clay". That Adamic man was formed from earth bound ingredients and at that time there was a lot of clay structure everywhere on Earth. The Hebrew word "Yahweh", was interpreted as Lord-God. And from the tertacarnation Yawed HV, the Hebrew word "Yahove, past, present, and future", that's what the phrase means, was interpreted as God. The bible is based on Hebrew-scholars-inscribed interpretations of oriental philosophy for chosen people which were to come. These scribes were called "masores" or "masorites" and they wrote what is called the Masoretic text. Therefore, we now have a universally-created, self-contained, parthenogenic, higher-consciousness God-created man, partially absorbed and identified on a single planet. An expressly lowered made entity, whose ability to reproduce itself as God was lost. Then a polarized mankind in which the divine principle separates in two distinct bodies, called male and female. This new and lesser creature was called by the ancient ones "human", under the God Huberous, or animal self, animal God which was depicted by the Sphinx. We now have found Sphinxes throughout the Earth and the Sphinx on the moon, and the Sphinx on Mars, all with hue-animal qualities. And since some look Negroid, and only a few look Caucasoid, we have a challenge of interpretation and possibly a need for great research.

I quote that in Genesis first and second chapters, "and it came to pass (which means after some time it passed) when man began to multiply on the face of the earth and daughters were born onto them, that the sons of God saw the daughters of men, that they were fair and took of them wise all of which they choose and was born to them mighty men, and there were giants in the earth".

Now, could any kind of logic be applied to that biblical reference? It means a primordial race of people born of God (Sons of God) had no daughters or distinctly separate females amongst them. So they took to themselves those completely polarized units, called females, that were on Earth and eventually lost the female quality within themselves and they were no longer hermaphrodites. They produced at first females. Later on, some males who were incomplete, were produced and continued to fight hard to propagate their kind through operative circumcision. Their prostrate tried to become a womb. And again, they had a shell over the penis, much as the clitoris has, and it had to be cut back to let this extended species exist as a self-contained person.

The male reproductive organs, called phallus, penis, prostate, and testes, scroctum, and orkick are similar to what is found in the females. The female fallopian tubes resemble the male vas deferens glands. The male prostate, not prostrate - prostrate is to prostrate oneself in front of on the ground or at a lower angle, prostate means "to stand in front of" alone. There also was a key which they hid from you. Every man has a rudimentary mammary gland of a female and can produce milk, and the bulbous urethra glands of the man are equal to the larger vestibular glands in women. The same thing that I stated, just backward, as when I gave "the woman lecture". The elongated clitoris, when stimulated and or genetically mutated, becomes the penis, and the testes found in the scrotum are nothing more than a descended ovum.

I repeat again, the keys are here, "prostate" means "to stand in front of", "prostrate" means "to lie flat with your face downward". The prostate gland stands in front of the male urethra and in front of the bladder and ahead of orkick gland. The reason man has prostrate troubles can be seen when you realize that the atrophied womb is not complete and the orckick gland, through its radiations, causes live sperm to be produced within that sac and makes a man separate from a womb man.

Understand this collective title "man" met an interactive species or a hermaphrodite that later on in the fall of man was called "Adam 2", a separate species with separate sexual reproductive organs. One following the menses of the animals of Earth. But if a man was a God-man, there are planets without moons, and consequently couldn't have mensing animals. Animals follow the cycle of an orbiting satellite. Man goes wherever the planet leads and he is free to go to the many classrooms in the heavens.

You didn't understand what I said, did you? How many did? That's beautiful. How many partially did, but are still thinking about it? How many didn't understand a thing I said at all, plus you don't want to expand your consciousness? Thank you for not raising your hand. Most men who are sons of God have a hole in the roof of their mouth just beyond the palate and up from the epithitimus gland that leads to the nasal eye duct. I'll repeat that simply. And women, if you are a real womb-man, you won't have that hole there. The men will have it. If you take your tongue, men, and put it near the roof of the mouth, near the teeth and move it backwards, it tickles. You will feel little ridges, little furloughs, and then a mound on the reverse or onverse side, going back toward the end of the throat near the larynx and again the palate. Up in the top, there is a lot of little soft tissue, then you will see a big mound and a little hole or entrance to that cave. That hole is either close or open and indented or big, depending on what kind of man you are. Now, let's take a whole minute, and do some homework in our mouths, men only, please. If you find it or already know of it, simply raise your hand. How many can't find it there at all? I'll have to talk to you. There is, again, a little soft, don't swallow, I don't want anyone to go into epileptic seizures. If you take your tongue and put it in the back of the mouth and bring it forward, you will see a little pithy area and a little hard area: it's right in the middle of that. Like a little mound. And right at the base there is a little indentation. Then you slide forward like going down a hill, you come forward to the teeth. How many men can, again, feel that area? Let me see your hands? That little open area leading on the reverse side of the mound or hill is what a lot of transposition and literature has tried to hide from you. It separates the two kinds of men on Earth and definitely separates hu-man from man. It is your ability to go through that channel up directly to the pituitary pineal gland. Once a month, as woman who has a menses, you have an issue of air or fluid that comes down there if you are in any way balanced. Most men not being told about it, don't do anything about it or don't even realize as what it can do or why it is happening. After a while, without proper nurturing, it becomes like an airflow and you may have noticed sometimes, even once or twice a week, especially when you are more rested and not under the stress of a job or business, air coming down there.

Just in passing, I would like to query my audience, like you query me. How many have heard that air coming down or bubbling or knew where it was coming down from or where? Ok. That separates the fallen man from the original man and hu–man, the animal portion from man which was non–solar. Solar plexus grounded man. Man himself may be incomplete in terms of understanding of who he is, and that the separation of man vs. human may be different. I state that man, mankind, and human may be different. The collective noun, in this case "man", may be different. The collective noun, in this case "man", may be dualistic. There are references in the biblical and also in scientific research that there was more than one kind of man, if you would. I has also talked about the various glands that men had and how they somewhat emulate what is found in a woman. But then we separate, to find that there is an organ that man has at the top of the mouth and the woman has no part of. Some men on Earth do not have it. Therefore, that is one way of defining and understanding that there are two kinds of species here that we call "man". One I would call "hu-man" and the other I would call "man". Looking at "man" itself, we now see "man with this divine cave". The legendary area in which a man may go into himself and find out his infinite being and open up many mansions of understanding as to who he is once he gets past what is called "the cross of cavalry" or "the crucification of the two thieves". The two thieves become the nnubo idapengala numagastic nerves at the base of the spine, ending up to the base of the neck, called the medulla stem. The thieves, therefore robbers, become this energy that is channeled backward down, to keep a man more to an animal state than to let him ascend to his higher consciousness and powers, becoming a God of a God himself.

When a man was said to become a fallen angel, it simply meant that man had fallen from the understanding of total consciousness, which makes him a co-creator on the thought plane. He was given a planet lower in thought, where this could not be practiced until he learned about what divine reality could bring. Therefore, on this planet he needed a mate, which was himself in the higher heavens. Now that may become difficult to stretch your minds to, but as I understand, in Philadelphia you are beginning to expand consciousness at a great level. So, I'd say that is the conclusion that I would reach for a man. To reach that conclusion for a man, however, is to also understand that the prostate gland itself, which receipts a rich vitamin A, vitamin E, and vitamin B complex, works hand and hand with the pineal gland. The pineal gland is best exercised at night at 10 PM and at 2:30 PM, especially on full moons.

This gland needs total darkness in order to regenerate itself and what is called the astral light. That light reflects down to the base of the man's spine, while he is in a sleep state. If the food intake has been rich in vitamin B complex, the plant kingdom's chlorophyll will also photosynthetically inundate the orkick gland, which then radiates upwards, and the man becomes one.

He becomes a living, walking psychic being. Internal emissions, some call them nocturnal emissions, are emissions used when that seed of light granted by the orkick gland is not raised up the spine, not used. Thus, the extrasensory perception which makes a man question his basic animal behavior. To do so is to raise man's consciousness to control one's dreams and control what is called the astral body. To not do so is to seat in the sperm, ready for reproduction, and this is where a man needed a mate. To live is to know temptations. The term "live" spelled backwards is "evil". The word "evil" transposed is "evil". To live is to go backward and become the devil. The word "devil" backwards is the word "lived".

Therefore, if one lives in evil and ignorance, one becomes a life of the devil. Man is his own worst devil and creates thin energy cycles, which then draw to them, from wherever in the heavens they dwell, negative beings termed devils.

Impotency is much a mental state in a man's mind as it is physical impotency. What a man sees, understands, and terms pictures from, he then brings to himself. What a man refuses to see or accept, he sends away from himself. Therefore, a man is surrounded by his own vibrations, and the vibrations he has in mind are the man himself.

Prostate, as I said before, means to stand in front of the gates of the higher heavens. Prostrate, as I said before, means a supplicant that gives you the physical confidence and physical bliss. The reason the sons of God or the angels, the energies from other planets, came to men is that Earth was really a divine garden, a wonderful co- mixture of everything from the planet Sirius, and the planet planet Orion, or the higher consciousness Orion, or the phylum consciousness in Palates.

Those two oppositions fought battles for the energies that have become man and woman on Earth to see who would take over the Garden of Eden. The planet Earth itself, one of the most beautiful planets in the cosmos, was used as a zoo or a deep genetic phylum for mutation, experimentation, and withdrawal.

Because man has fallen here on Earth, the progress of souls through the higher heavens has stopped feeding from the solar system, and man is bottlenecked with many energies and entities, which we now call devils or lower energies. To stop that bottleneck and let Earth change is another problem and a challenge.

The species that wants men not to progress will also do everything to keep the man an animal and to bring more out of his animal side. Then there are the species who want men to become as they are and even more, as they have sustained the trails of time. Time is supposedly different on Earth. The latter species want men to break the bonds of animalness and rise and ascend.

The time of all of this, speculated by many good books and bad authors, is not in the distant future, but upon us now. The weather changes and the weather patterns that we see indicate this. The ozone layer peels back so that direct light can come from the central sun, which will kill off all that is of lower vibrations and reign down the diseases of animals in which partook.

The conclusion can only be changed by the mind of men, when they will understand. If man refuses to act, then hu-man will be destroyed from the surface of Earth.

Thus ends the man lecture. It is open for questions and comments. Not to forget there is still a children lecture to follow.

The Real Man, Woman, and Child Lecture

Part 4

I'd like to move on from the concept of man. But I left one thing out. I don't know how I could do that. But things happen. So, consequently, I want to correct that. In finishing the woman lecture, I gave you only one gland that was erroneously reported and that is the three-lobed thyroid rather than the two-lobed thyroid. The three-lobed thyroid belongs to women. What is not talked about at all are two of the female glands that are still there, one in an almost atrophied state, and one that can be renewed.

To preface that, I'd like to give a whole minute talk about mitochondrial DNA. This is for those who want proof and for those others who are on the border line. Then you'd have to study mitochondrial DNA and nuclear DNA. Nuclear DNA is a mixture of both parents, both parents genes. Mitochondrial DNA is an inherited genre from just one of them, and that is the mother. It is altered by mediation. When that happens, it leads to racial differences. They now can genetically prove there is one mitochondrial DNA that may be of the mother of all human life on Earth, but for nuclear DNA it takes radiation to bring that out.

When radiation enters upon the womb, then certain glands in the womb begin to undergo mitosis on their own. This is why for a long time, women were told to avoid direct sunlight and especially moonlight, which could have caused mitosis on a lower energy level.

The two glands are the following ones: the epoophoron, found between the uterus and the ovary, and the paroophron. The latter one produces seminal fluid and seminal secretions, just like a male would. It is found below the massus suffix. That concludes the woman lecture.

And dealing with the final lecture tonight, that of children, I must say I find it to be probably one of the most interesting. That's because a child is what is called an incomplete being, one that is waiting for maturity to become a male or female, a man or a woman. That state in-between is when each soul undergoes a change, having the opportunity to learn from those who have either previously misused it or didn't know about it.

"Children", or what they used to call "kinters", entering kindergarten or the little zoo garden of the Earth, in many cases came from distant areas or planets and needed to learn what it is to find eagerness and what the physical reality is. They journeyed so long in the heavenly thought planes, they found just very few planets willing to accept them and not completely hurt them by experiencing physical reality.

The mother and father, combining in physical thoughts as well as physical coitus, generate energies by which these thoughts form, based on their level of radiation drawn into the cycle of birth. Therefore, the time of coitus and union is important if it is meant to propagate life on a planet such as Earth.

Drugs, and anything like drugs that curtail the ability of the soul to know the Self at the time of conception, pull in lower energies, without question. That is why drugs are not necessary and many souls who made their entrance on the drugged mind were stopped from becoming great.

Thus the doctor's recommendation of not doing drugs while having copious coitus, as lower entities could come into our planet uncontrolled. They had come and they had brought forth their kind. These unchecked children are now the scientists of the present day, with very little spiritual insight, because they had parents with very little wisdom. As a consequence, now these Earth-bound souls are holding back the progression of this planet. They came in at a time when Earth needed to have no souls bound, but the freest thinking and most spiritual ones, in order to upgrade the planetary vibrations and stop the Earth from being annihilated.

It's just that simple. Those who ducked out from Sirius must now stand for themselves, as they have lost their abilities and earths where to breed. They are on their way out. They are coming back one more time to try and rectify that, by luring you to accept their souls and make children of their breeding, so that they will have a place to stay.

It's just that simple. The souls that you now call children are probably older than you, and have wisdom beyond you. But they didn't have a chance to prove it. When you don't have to fight an enemy, you can bring out a lot. Even in battle you must come off of theory and get practical. They look for the practice here on Earth, one of the best planets to bring in physical reality to a norm. These children have a lot to teach you, but they must first be guided to unlock their reservoirs of regenerative energy, which we call psychic patterns, through what is called reliving the past lives. That or through the birth canal, when they talk directly to the carrier, or mother, or through psychical sight, which unlocks the little programs hidden in the subconscious, which we call the right brain.

Not only will that make everybody more honest and more psychic, but it will stop the entrance of lower vibratory individuals in this world. That is because those souls would respect coitus, and would understand that there is a need for mind control going along with it.

They will fight to the death to stop harsh creatures from proliferating, and therefore they seek guidance. If the guidance comes from you, the parent, they will accept it. If it comes from the State they will not accept it, and the state will have a showdown.

But the State knows that they come here as warriors, because it is ignorant of the truth. People who were lied to before coming to Earth could not graduate to higher heavens and further classroom teachings. They resented what happened to them and became very angry and would also want to return here quickly. The tape drugs and the astral will explain to you about the four levels of the astral plane and the higher levels of mental planes, and the odic plane.

I can only say without staying here for 3 or 4 more hours, or 3 or 4 more days, which you wouldn't want me to do anyway, that the souls are old. There are no new souls being created to enter into the planet Earth's density. They are here for re-learning, or to exercise the truth they think is real, and they look at you for guidance to destroy you.

They are strong. They do not accept weakness, they do not understand weakness, and in many cases they are very angry that they are here in the first place. Without direction, you are building an army for the evil negativities, referred to as the devil. With direction, you are building the umbilical cord for the angels to transit to Lira and to Sirius, beyond the Cosmos and to the pure thought realms.

They can make you better, but they challenge you, because they make you be right. They make you think and they take time. If you don't have time, don't bring them in. In conclusion, I simply state this:

what you have heard tonight is different, what you have heard tonight rings bells that you know are true, and for others rings bells that say "take a break".

To kind of summate what I said, I would like you to stand by me to read three poems. They summate what I have said to you in prose. One is called simply "Mother Earth". In this age of unisex, neutered gender and the like, it really no longer matters where the bar rests on the bike. Hetero and homo are not adjectives, but nouns. As we really start to look at it, it can be quite profound to imagine Earth had a mother. Imagine that in case of an attempt of hurting her offspring, she would go very wild. Now we say we are God's children and that he watches over us, but if he is still fitted with mother, it may be a cause of fuss. By calling Earth our "mother", we may be offending a he.

Now, I saw a reversing of polarity in 1959. Yet, if we really ponder this situation, it can become complexly mad if Earth were to change its sex. We can lose what we never had. I hope this is not too confusing for you. I don't know if the sons of Gods were heterosexual, I truly don't know the answer, for we each must find our own truth. On the other hand, I have been taught that without mothers and dads there can be no youth. Yet maybe that is the answer in crystal clarity.

For if we offend no one's mother, and no one's dad, we may al reach polarity. Thank You!

A man once sat in the garden of life and studied first the Sun, and then the Moon. While enraptured by splendors, he prayed for balance, hoping she would come soon. A woman attracted by Earth's blue-green globe, magnetically entered its gate, and then decided to take a tour. She was going where her longing heart craved for her mate, looking towards the heavens. They both realized all parts must be one, burning and growing inside to be a whole, and yet sons of the Sun. For each comet, fortress, sphere, galaxy, cosmos, and nebulae only led them to understand that their creator was near, stripping them of ego and the personal eye.

As in Nature, whose rhythms and balances flow, making love to all those of higher and lower energy levels, humans must find their mates, if they ever are to find their heaven. And now on Earth it is truly possible to see the balance that love brings to all of us. Us, the ones who make mistakes till we search deep within for ourselves - the best mate of them all.

Finding the summation, Hu-man. Oh, magnificent beast, on this strange and enchanted land, you roam your asphalt jungle clothed in skin that we call man: insensitive, incredulous, and incongruous to all God's creative works that you find both large and small. Just how long can you travel in yourself? You have lied about history by distortion, deletion, deception, and disguise. You have altered rich records to our skies. You have reconstructed universes and even hell and there seems to be no end to the lies your mouth can tell! What you view and grasp imprisons what you see. So you distort the very heavens. You will change even the smallest beasts. There is nothing you wouldn't do in order for your fame to increase, yet you know within yourself that your time is running out and your life must end soon.

As we view each bright new morning, although through polluted skies, we know there is a creator, for creation never lies. Thus, we come together, knowing that aging is a blessing from our creator and a divine release from you.

I thank you and good night!

PLEASE UNIVERSAL CREATOR

KNOW IN MY HEART THAT I LOVE YOU.

PLEASE PROTECT ME AND THIS PLANET ON WHICH I LIVE NOW!

PLEASE OPEN MY MIND, MY SPIRIT AND MY SOUL TO RECEIVE ONLY TRUTH AND YOUR LOVE NOW!

Join millions of others: recite this prayer at 12-noon and at sunset daily! It ma also be recited anytime you feel the need for mental and spiritual strength. Directed prayer via concentrated mental focusing will create a spiritual calmness and balance which will strengthen your physical immune system! "We fight not against flesh an blood but against principalities and spiritual wickedness in high places..."

May the Creator Bless All Good People Everywhere.

www.ingramcontent.com/pod-product-compliance
Lightning Source LLC
LaVergne TN
LVHW011431080426
835512LV00005B/384